I. C. JARVIE

# Functionalism

A SERIES ON
BASIC CONCEPTS IN ANTHROPOLOGY
Under the Editorship of
A. J. Kelso, University of Colorado
Aram Yengoyan, University of Michigan

# Functionalism

I. C. JARVIE
York University, Toronto

Burgess Publishing Company ● Minneapolis, Minnesota

# Introduction to Functional Explanation

*Thou shalt not eat any abominable thing ... the swine, because it divideth the hoof, yet cheweth not the cud, it is unclean unto you: ye shall not eat of their flesh, nor touch their dead carcase.*

—*Deuteronomy, 14, 3 and 8*

The Jewish (and Islamic) taboo on eating pork is an example of a custom with no very obvious explanation. This makes it typical of the problems wrestled with by anthropologists. To taboo *that* meat rather than *this* (and a rather tasty that, at that), strikes some thinkers as *arbitrary* and hence *irrational*. Eighty years ago, such would have been the position of most anthropologists (e.g., W. Robertson Smith,[1] or J.G. Frazer) and they would doubtless have added that whatever brought it about is lost to us in the mists of prehistory. If this is any explanation at all, it is certainly not a very enlightening one.

Other writers shrink from dismissing taboos as arbitrary and irrational, suggesting instead that taboos such as that on pork stem from ancient (and now lost) rules of hygiene and uncleanliness (the pig being thought of as dirty, disease-ridden, dangerous in hot climates, etc.). There is no evidence to support this explanation in Deuteronomy or the corresponding passages in Leviticus. Moses Maimonides, writing in the twelfth century, and managing to find hygiene explanations for all the other dietary taboos of Mosaic law, could not find one for pork. Instead he advanced the *aesthetic* argument that pork is forbidden because of the revolting diet and habits of the domestic pig. So, if there was an ancient system of hygiene that explains the pork taboo, it

---

[1] William Robertson Smith (1846-1894) was expelled from the Free Church College of Aberdeen on grounds of heresy and later was professor of Arabic at the University of Cambridge. Along with the lawyer Sir Henry Maine (1822-1888) and the philosopher Herbert Spencer (1820-1903), he was one of the handful of nineteenth century precursors of the functional approach in the social sciences.

*shares these distinctive characters and is therefore of the same general species. This is a kind of casuistry which permits scope for hunting antelope and wild goats and wild sheep. Everything would be quite straightforward were it not that the legal mind has seen fit to give ruling on some borderline cases. Some animals seem to be ruminant such as the hare and the hyrax. . . . But they are definitely not cloven-hoofed. . . . Similarly for animals which are cloven-hoofed but are not ruminant, the pig and the camel. Note that this failure to conform to the two necessary criteria for defining cattle is the only reason given in the Old Testament for avoiding the pig; nothing whatever is said about its dirty scavenging habits. As the pig does not yield milk, hide nor wool, there is no other reason for keeping it except for its flesh. And if the Israelites did not keep pig they would not be familiar with its habits. I suggest that originally the sole reason for its being counted as unclean is its failure as a wild boar to get into the antelope class, and that in this it is on the same footing as the camel and the hyrax. . . . (pp. 54-55).*

It should be apparent at once that we have here an explanation of the taboo on pork that is far superior to anything that has gone before. It locates the taboo within a *context* of ideas and practices which *make systematic sense*. It assumes that the taboo is to be explained by the way the society is, not the society by the taboos it has.

All these points are characteristic of functional explanation in its sophisticated modern form. As we shall see, it, too, is vulnerable to criticism. But a measure of its intellectual superiority over previous types of explanation is that these arguments will take many pages to state. Whatever hard things are later said of functionalism, because of it anthropology is decisively different in its whole approach to problems like taboo, and that approach is vastly superior to what went before.

✗ We have approached functionalism by means of a concrete problem in anthropology rather than attempting to encapsulate it in a definition because, strictly speaking, there is no such thing as functionalism. There have been and still are diverse anthropologists who could be called functionalists (although some would disavow the label). But the fact that they put forward functional explanations to meet anthropological problems was not sufficient to form them into a unified group or party. Such subgroups as once clustered round rival functionalist teachers like B. Malinowski and A.R. Radcliffe-Brown disintegrated soon after their leaders' demise — if they had not done so before. So, rather than seek spurious clarity by introducing functionalism by definition, we shall come at it as an episode in the history of anthropology; an episode which makes up with richness of genuine scientific debate for what is lost in conceptual tidiness of definitions.

Having looked at functionalism in a strong and plausible form we shall now proceed as follows. In the chapter "Beginnings and Development," we shall go back to the founders of functionalism in anthropology, Malinowski and Radcliffe-Brown. From the start it will be apparent that there are differences as well as similarities between them. Their own subsequent development will be noted, as will what seem like important contributions by others. Then in the chapter on "Modification Under Criticism" we will turn to the critical debate which has centered around functionalism since 1935, showing how its mistakes were gradually exposed, and how its strengths were brought out and developed. Finally, we will attempt an "Assessment."

# Beginnings and Development

Conventionally, functionalist ideas are traced back to the group of French thinkers around *L'Année Sociologique* at the turn of the century, and especially Emile Durkheim and Henri Hubert.[4] But to seek continuity in the history of ideas by searching out the antecedents for every idea makes the history of ideas look altogether too smooth. The alternative is to begin at a relatively arbitrary point and try to make sense of what is going on then. We shall begin in 1922 with the first anthropologist to declare himself a functionalist, Bronislaw Malinowski.[5] Whenever a doctrine is produced, as Malinowski produced functionalism in 1922, it helps if we sketch the problem-situation into which it enters.

The year 1922 saw the publication of Malinowski's first major report on his fieldwork in Melanesia, which he called *Argonauts of the Western Pacific*. The problem he set himself was to explain a remarkable phenomenon he had come across in the Trobriand Islands: the *kula*. This was a curious pattern of ceremonial trade which connected the islands together; in fact the islands exchanging goods with each other made up a complete circle. What was special was that this trade was regarded as very important, with specially organized expeditions, elaborate ceremonial and boats, the whole business obviously invested with great significance. And yet, what was actually traded (or swapped) were two quite inessential kinds of objects: necklaces made of red shell and bracelets made of white shell. The sole use made of these objects seemed to be in this trading, and, moreover, necklaces were always swapped for bracelets and *vice versa*. Other and more practical kinds of trade might

---

[4] Emile Durkheim (1858-1917) was professor of philosophy at the University of Bordeaux, and founder and editor of *L'Année Sociologique,* which ran from 1898-1914. Henri Hubert (1872-1927) was a close collaborator of Durkheim.

[5] Bronislaw Malinowski (1884-1942) was born in Poland and received his PhD in physics from the University of Cracow in 1908. Upon reading Frazer's *The Golden Bough,* he decided to study anthropology at the London School of Economics, where he became professor in 1927. During his last few years he taught mainly at Yale.

take place coincidentally, but they were not part of the *kula*. Since the groups trading were essentially the representatives of one island visiting another, and since each side only traded either necklaces or bracelets, the result was that these ceremonial objects circulated around the ring of *kula* islands.

What could the explanation of this apparently pointless trading of value-less objects be? Trading of products, food, salt, or knick-knacks makes perfect sense. But what of these elaborate and costly expeditions, over many miles of ocean, occurring quite regularly and surrounded by great ceremonial — what could the explanation of them be? That knick-knacks should be traded on the side of more important trading is understandable enough; but when the whole megillah centers around knick-knacks, the anthropologist is set to wondering. The necklaces and bracelets are not even kept; what is received is soon passed on in another trade. Moreover, there is prestige surrounding the *kula:* only certain men can conduct the trading, and once in that position, they keep it.

What, then, is the explanation Malinowski offers? "The *kula* is thus an extremely big and complex institution. . . . It welds together a considerable number of tribes, and it embraces a vast complex of activities, interconnected, and playing into one another, so as to form one organic whole" (1922, p. 83). So what the *kula* does, according to Malinowski, is organize: it "welds," "embraces" the islands into an "organic whole." Malinowski believes he has explained the *kula* by showing, in the course of his lengthy book, how the economic and ceremonial aspects of culture "functionally depend on one another" (1922, p. 515).

This functional explanation is not going to satisfy someone who comes asking, "Why do the Trobrianders have the *kula*?" That kind of problem demands an historical answer, which, like the origins of the pork taboo, may be lost in the mists of time. Similarly, to ask why they do what they do demands an answer in terms of custom and tradition amounting to little more than saying they were brought up that way. Malinowski is really answering a quite different kind of question: what is the social significance, for Trobriand society, of having the *kula*? What *function* does the *kula* perform? The assumption, clearly, is that the *kula* is not there by *accident*; it doesn't just happen; it is socially significant. But what does "socially significant" mean? It means, "serves some function for the society." What function? The function of welding the society together into an organic whole. So is revealed another component idea of functionalism, that societies consist of institutional parts welded together. Behind this idea ultimately lurks the problem of social order: How is social order possible, and how is social order maintained? Malinowski might be interpreted as saying, the *kula* trading ring is a means of maintaining social order amongst a group of widely scattered Melanesian societies. It should be noted that he is not offering an explanation of how the *kula* is possible. For that, we must turn to the work of another English scholar, A.R. Radcliffe-Brown.[6]

In 1922, the same year that saw Malinowski's *Argonauts*, Radcliffe-Brown published his first book *The Andaman Islanders*. The book went rapidly out of print, as Radcliffe-Brown's work never caught on with the general public as Malinowski's did. However, his influence in the scholarly world was to be much greater, partly perhaps because of his later work. The beginnings of the functionalist approach as he saw it are clearly presaged in the Andaman volume. The book is an attempt to explain the religious myths and ceremonies of the Andaman Islanders. Radcliffe-Brown recalls that originally he set out to explain them by reconstructing the history of the society but that, perhaps because of the paucity of historical material in a preliterate society and the consequent need of much conjecture for its reconstruction, perhaps because of what he expected an explanation to do, the results proved unenlightening. Instead, he decided to look for the significance or the function of the religious customs rather than their origins. In a preface to the 1932 re-issue of his book, he quotes the French sociologist Henri Hubert enjoining the sociologist to ignore the *content* of religious beliefs and to concentrate on their *effects*. Society is not the way it is because of religious ideas; religious ideas are what they are because of society. Radcliffe-Brown says he accepts the idea that society depends for its existence on a system of sentiments which regulate the conduct of the individual in accord with the needs of society. Religious ceremonies are a means of giving collective expression to these sentiments, hence reinforcing them and transmitting them from one generation to the next. Hence their "social function" is their effect on the solidarity or cohesion of the society.

This is a theory both of how social order is maintained, and of how it is possible. It is possible because the natural conflicts between men are regulated and controlled by the organization of the society, which also fosters sentiments to control this conflict. The assumptions here are, first, that there exists social harmony and social continuity and, second, that it is these that have to be explained. There are those who claim that men would naturally harmonize with each other were not the sentiments induced by organized society perverting this tendency. Continuity, also, might be held to be both precarious and hardly in need of explanation; on the contrary, it might be claimed: a species that has survived this far in evolution has done so by adapting itself to the environment, by changing; by defending itself against its natural enemies which change, bringing on changed adaptations.

Be all that as it may, we can see that in these early works of Radcliffe-Brown and Malinowski there has emerged a way of explaining social institu-

---

[6] A.R. Radcliffe-Brown (1881-1955) taught anthropology at Cape Town, Sydney, Chicago, Oxford, and Alexandria.

tions which is interesting and enlightening and on which the two anthropologists converged at almost the same time. These two functionalists (a label Malinowski invented and Radcliffe-Brown always repudiated) developed the concept of function in divergent ways subsequently, and their pupils were noticeably different on this account.

Malinowski was a flamboyant, perhaps even charismatic, figure, whose main influence was in encouraging pupils to go out and do fieldwork. However, those among them who became anthropologists usually turned for theoretical guidance to the more rigorous Radcliffe-Brown. So, while Malinowski almost single-handedly popularized anthropology within academe, and while he influenced a great many (including, incidentally, the sociologist Talcott Parsons, who studied with him in 1924), in the end the direction taken by anthropology, and more especially by functionalism, was not of his making.

Twenty years after *Argonauts* appeared Malinowski was to be dead. They were prolific years, during which his conception of function changed radically. The influence of Durkheim and French sociology which was so strong in the early years appears to have waned, although it is not clear why. My suggestion would be that Malinowski's functionalism bore only on the problem of the persistence of society, and not on the problem of how social order is possible. His functional theory of the *kula* admirably shows how diverse aspects of one society connect up into a harmonious and hence persisting (since not internally disrupted[7]) system. It does not, however, account for how this system comes to be where it is, how it is possible at all. When discussing this problem, Malinowski sets aside functionalism and gives an evolutionary explanation: social life is possible because it is an adaptive mechanism, by means of which man copes with his environment, that is to say, satisfies his basic needs as a biological organism. In order to get food, rest, shelter, clothing, mates, etc., it is necessary for man to organize, and the societies we presently confront are, as it were, the survivors of possibly many experiments at devising such adaptive mechanisms. Thus, no particular form of social organization was seen as necessary to human life, but the viable social forms are those which managed to supply these basic needs. Society is thus both possible and necessary because of man's (social) biology.

We can now look at some consequences of this relatively novel social biological mode of explanation. These may help explain why Malinowski moved further and further in this direction as time went on, getting further

---

[7] This qualification is important. Functionalism explains the persistence of systems. Extra-systemic factors are excluded. But such extra-systemic events as earthquakes, wars of other nations, and changes in the terms of trade can wreak havoc with the society's persistence. The devout functionalist will counter this argument by suggesting such cataclysms are themselves parts of wider systems which may in their turn be susceptible of functional analysis.

and further away from the functionalism of Durkheim to which he was originally close.

(1) One consequence of this mode of argument was that currently existing societies could not be treated as living fossils, preserved specimens of earlier forms of social life. It is hard to imagine how strongly prevalent was this view which Malinowski attacked. Indeed, in spite of his great influence, even today one can find journalists referring to Stone Age societies in New Guinea, The Philippines, Brazil. As Malinowski has taught us, this is an error. For if a society has survived into the twentieth century, obviously it is adapted to the twentieth century; moreover, there is no way of knowing to what extent, if at all, a contemporaneous society resembles such social forms as may have been around in the early days of mankind's history. So why speculate that any of them do? We have no way of checking (and thus improving on) our speculations. All we can know is how the society is now.[8] So, Malinowski argued, our most promising line of inquiry into diverse societies is into how they are and how they work *now*. Unlike the remote past, these societies are here now and we can directly develop our ideas and explanations against a living reality. This is the exercise known as intensive fieldwork.

Malinowski's attitude to fieldwork was quite new. He changed it from an interesting thing an anthropologist might do if he felt so inclined, but which he could just as well leave to correspondents or assistants, to making it the heart of what it is to be an anthropologist, the paradigm of what it was to do anthropology. Unless one had oneself gone through the exercise of leaving behind one's own society and entering into a totally different one, it was not possible to grasp the total reality of alternative social systems — or so he argued. From cataloguing the exotic, which was what much of earlier anthropology consisted in, anthropology became confrontation with, followed by acceptance of, and, ultimately, understanding of the ways of life of other people.[9] This attitude in a compelling teacher succeeded in transforming anthropology in Malinowski's lifetime.

(2) Another consequence of Malinowski's social biology was this. Any living society is viable, but it is not the only viable society. Hence, though the *kula* may make the Trobriand Islands viable, perhaps other forms of social organization could also sustain them. So, it is not enough to explain the *kula* to show how it keeps the Islands knitted together into a system. The explana-

---

[8] Here Malinowski is in error. There are strong arguments to show that earliest man was a hunter and gatherer, not a nomad or pastoralist, still less a horticulturalist. This granted it can be argued that certain very ramified and extensive (over both space and time) forms of social organization are not possible amongst early mankind.

[9] While often justified by appeal to methodological arguments about the need to collect a data base for anthropology, willingness to do fieldwork also had strong moral overtones.

tion is not complete. Malinowski seems not to have noticed this difficulty.

(3) Indeed, survival shows fitness, not the greatest possible fitness. Darwin's survival of the fittest is of the fittest around, not of the fittest possible. Hence, that a society knitted together by the *kula* is fit, does not show that it is the fittest possible.

Radcliffe-Brown agreed wholeheartedly with (1). He was as blind as Malinowski about (2) which could be levelled against his functionalism also. Both anthropologists were criticized along the lines of (3) in their lifetimes and both were ambivalent. The next step in the argument of (3) is to suggest that conscious reform or change might even improve the fitness of the society. Unfortunately, the fieldworking anthropologist, having confronted, accepted, and finally understood a complex social system, is not sure that tampering will improve it. Men may not always know what havoc they wreak. The ravages of colonialism and wage labour were plain to the anthropologist in the South Seas and Africa. Yet, say what they would, these processes would go on. So it was easy for anthropologists to talk themselves into advising both the natives and the powers that be with the result that they themselves did not know where they were.

In all this, the influence of the two men runs parallel, despite Radcliffe-Brown's objections to Malinowski's social biology. A clue to why Radcliffe-Brown opposed social biology emerges in his rejection of Malinowski's functional explanation of magic. Malinowski argued that magic served the *psychological* function of being a means of reducing anxiety in situations where there is an element of chance or hazard, especially misfortune. This was the sort of thing a strict functionalist such as Radcliffe-Brown, who took his sociologism directly from the French school, was bound to repudiate. Social life, for Durkheim, was *sui generis.* Reduction, whether of social processes to biological needs or of social processes to psychological needs, was consistently rejected. Radcliffe-Brown was true to his lights.

This may be why Radcliffe-Brown gained a kind of intellectual influence never matched by Malinowski. He, too, was for fieldwork and against speculative historical reconstruction, but more than either of these, his functionalism maintained that society was *sui generis,* had to be studied on its own level and explained in its own terms. It is this aspect of functionalism, which we certainly owe to Durkheim, that may account for its being incorporated into sociology and social anthropology in such a way that it will never be abandoned. The philosophical premises of functional analysis may be, indeed probably have been, abandoned; but that living social facts have to be treated on their own terms, that cannot be abandoned without abandoning the sociological enterprise itself. This point also goes some way to account for the differences between British and American anthropology, for, whereas the British were more than content to allow a complete continuum between sociology and social anthropology, the Americans were not. Franz Boas,

Alfred Kroeber, *et al.,* were on their way to developing a non-sociological science of man, combining archeological, physiological, and cultural materials, long before sociological functionalism appeared in 1922. It may not surprise us, then, that they found it unnecessary and did not voluntarily change their whole style of anthropology by accepting it.

Although Radcliffe-Brown's own fieldwork was sporadic and scrappy, he was indefatigable as a teacher. After several years as a professor in South Africa and then Australia, he betook himself to the University of Chicago where, from 1931-1937, he exerted great influence but more in that he trained a group of students rather than that he changed the whole face of the subject. As we shall see, resistance to his functionalism remained strong in America, and polemics were to come — despite Eggan's (1955) attempts to fuse the two approaches.

Unlike Malinowski, who spent most of his life writing up field material and throwing out what amounted to theoretical "asides," Radcliffe-Brown spent his remaining thirty-three years after *The Andaman Islanders* appeared in teaching and developing his theoretical ideas, most clearly expounded in the papers which constitute *Structure and Function in Primitive Society* (1952). Reflecting on such problems as why certain Australian aboriginal societies are divided into two, four, or even eight segments for the purpose of marriage-partner selection, or the peculiar status of the mother's brother in several South African Bantu societies, or so-called "joking relationships" between relatives, Radcliffe-Brown was able to exemplify his Durkheimian ideas. He argued that the key to these peculiar customs was to be found in their social function, the ways in which they connected up with, and lent mutual support to, other features of the society.

This becomes clear if we look at his paper on "Taboo." Radcliffe-Brown did not address himself directly to the subject of the taboo on pork, but he did give a general theory which we can work out for pork. His theory tells us to seek the meaning and social function of such ritual avoidances as food taboos.

*... taboos relating to the animals and plants used for food are means of affixing a definite social value to food, based on its social importance. The* **social** *importance of food is not that it satisfies hunger, but that ... an enormously large proportion of ... activities are concerned with the getting and consuming of food, and that in these activities, with their daily instances of collaboration and mutual aid, there continuously occur those interrelations of interests which bind the individual men, women and children into a society (1952, p. 151).*

To affix a social value to food by prohibiting some hardly singles out pork and the other creatures banned in Mosaic law. So in this founder of functionalism, writing in 1939, we find an explanation vulnerable to the same criticism as some of the explanations with which we began this module. But what we should be taking note of here is not such specific shortcomings, but the way Radcliffe-Brown connects taboo to the collaboration and interrelation which bind people into a society.

Radcliffe-Brown stuck to a conception of society as an organic whole, its diverse parts mutually adjusted to, and fully integrated with, each other. Hence social features appeared peculiar only on first sight; upon closer inspection (especially or ideally through fieldwork) they could be seen as integral parts of the whole social system. This, he thought, was a scientific approach to the study of society; therefore he rejected as unenlightening all historical, psychological, environmental, evolutionary, or biological explanations. He pressed this point further. What such a scientific approach disclosed was that there were underlying patterns or principles in each social organization. Such unchanging patterns of relationships he came to call the social structure. It was his hypothesis that if the social structures of societies were compared it would be possible to classify them into a small number of groups and discover the general principles governing their operation. These would be the laws of a scientific anthropology. The main area of anthropology in which he attempted this was kinship. In particular he claimed to have discovered principles such as the solidarity of the lineage and the solidarity of the sibling group which were always present in unilineal descent societies. His work was carried forward by Fortes (1953) in his important paper "The Structure of Unilineal Descent Groups." Little has been done on the principles of non-unilineal kinship, except in the area of a taxonomy of kinship terminologies. The other main area in which principles of social structure have been sought out is politics and social control.

Because he was weak at this level of theory, Malinowski's influence tended to wane once fieldwork was over. Once the anthropologist was back in his study digesting, writing-up, and trying to explain what he had observed, the thought of Radcliffe-Brown came into its own. After all, Radcliffe-Brown postulated that there was an order in social life, there was a structure, and there were principles underlying that structure. An anthropologist thus had at his fingertips a scheme of questions and answers around which to organize his material. He could then fit his piece of local ethnography into various comparative schemes. Hence the staying power of Radcliffe-Brown's functionalist outlook with working anthropologists, long after the substantial theories which undergird that outlook had been severely criticized. Malinowski's functionalism provided nothing similar — to say that everything connects up makes for fat notebooks and organizational headaches. Not very enlightening.

In addition to helping organize fieldwork results, Radcliffe-Brown's functionalism had a revelatory character. We have already seen Radcliffe-Brown heeding Hubert's advice to look at what people do rather than what they say.

This was refined and gradually came out as: the contrast between what people say and what they do is of the greatest anthropological interest. They may say inheritance proceeds in this and this way, or that a person who belongs to that kinship group should marry such and such a relative. But with what frequency do they do this? If there are discrepancies between what people are supposed to do and what they actually do, how are these sustained (how are children reconciled to them) and why are they sustained (why are ideal and practice not brought into line)? This sort of question has led to an anthropologist actually observing a lineage in the process of rewriting its genealogies. If it is maintained that only a certain number of generations have passed since the time of the founder, sooner or later some generations are going to have to be "forgotten" or merged in order that the "correct" number of generations is preserved.

So it was not only its endorsement of fieldwork that commended functionalism to anthropologists but the sorts of questions it alerted anthropologists to ask. Whether or not the theory is abandoned, it is pretty sure that such valuable and revealing heuristic tools will not be.

Functionalism was to change little over the years. In 1940 E.E. Evans-Pritchard,[10] who was to succeed Radcliffe-Brown as Professor of Social Anthropology at Oxford University, published *The Nuer,* a study of kinship and social organization that has come to be cited as a paradigm of the sort of functionalism Radcliffe-Brown espoused. The main problem in the book is how Nuer society holds together although segments of it are constantly feuding and there are no chiefs. Evans-Pritchard's argument is that the extent of feuding is strictly regulated by kinship ties, which ensure that it never gets out of hand and becomes a war of all against all. The clue lay in lineages. A lineage is all those who trace their descent to a common ancestor through one "line" — male or female. So all the male descendants of a man are a lineage, as are all the female descendants of a woman. Since every man is potentially a lineage head (unless he has no sons), we can see that a branching or segmentary process develops. In Figure 1, A and D are lineages, B, C, E, and F are segments. If $B_1$ is feuding with $B_2$ no one but their own families and descendants is concerned. But if $B_2$ starts feuding with $C_1$, $B_1$ will take sides with $B_2$, as all members of lineage segment B stick together against lineage segment C. Similarly if $B_1$ feuds with $F_2$ the line-up will be ($B_1$, $B_2$, $C_1$, and $C_2$) *versus* ($E_1$, $F_1$, and $F_2$). (Incidentally, $E_1$ and G are the sorts of persons ripe to be merged out of a genealogy.) Similarly, all Nuer will stand together when it comes to harassing their neighboring tribe, the Dinka. Nuer society was especially interesting because it was the first with no political leaders or

---

[10] Sir Edward E. Evans-Pritchard (1902-     ), a student of Malinowski who did extensive fieldwork in North Africa, recently retired from a professorship of anthropology at the University of Oxford.

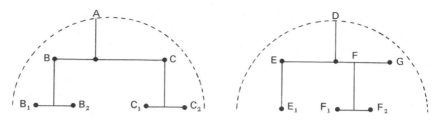

**Figure 1**

chiefs to be closely analyzed, so that the basis of its organization and cohesion could be understood.

In 1945 two sociologists, Kingsley Davis and Wilbert E. Moore, published a functional explanation of social stratification which also came to be cited as a paradigm of the method at work. At its crudest, their argument is that social stratification is a functional necessity because not all the tasks that need to be performed in a society are equally pleasant, equally easy, equally important to social survival. Roughly, stratification, or a system of status and rewards, is a filter to help ensure that the right people get into the right jobs and that they are then given social rewards for doing them properly. Stratification is, of course, only one form of reward: there are others, such as wealth, power, greater sexual opportunity, and so on.

— The next development within functionalism also came from a sociologist, Robert K. Merton,[11] who, in 1949, published *Social Theory and Social Structure,* which contained an important first chapter expanded out of earlier ideas of his. Its title was "Manifest and Latent Functions." This wide-ranging essay, which was further expanded and developed in the 1957 edition of the book, began by pointing out that a custom or institution could have two analytically distinct functions: overt or manifest, such as the function of marriage to beget children, of films to provide entertainment, of welfare to alleviate poverty; and covert or latent, such as the function of the *kula* to bind together a chain of islands, or of the pork taboo to encourage the integrity of the pastoralist way of life, or of the Nuer lineage in maintaining social cohesion in a feuding society, or the function of social class in ensuring that those most suited to them will get the crucial jobs in society.

The importance of this essay was to make it crystal clear that manifest functions were of little interest to the anthropologist. However, rather like the contrast between what people say and what they do, the contrast between what institutions are manifestly about, and what they are actually or

---

[11] Robert K. Merton (1910-    ) has taught sociology at Columbia University for many years.

additionally about, can be most interesting. The manifest function of the *kula* is to trade necklaces and bracelets; its latent function, as we have seen, is something else. The manifest function of Nuer lineages is to regulate marriage, descent, and inheritance; their latent function includes preventing feuds from splitting the society apart.

During World War II, functionalism became dominant in British anthropology, and it began to gain ground in American sociology. Following quickly upon Merton's book came, in 1951, Talcott Parsons'[12] *The Social System,* which combines functionalism with Weber and Simmel's action theory, and Marion J. Levy's[13] *The Structure of Society* in 1952. The latter, which attempts to lay down five basic functional requisites for a society to survive moves some way back towards the Malinowskian anchor in social evolution.

We cannot but see the forties and fifties as the high points of functionalist achievement: the major books appeared, the major writers rose to ascendency in the academic ranks. As an arbitrary high point I will select 1959, as the year in which Kingsley Davis,[14] in his presidential address to the American Sociological Association, developed his view of "The Myth of Functional Analysis as a Special Method in Sociology and Anthropology." The myth is that there is a special and homogeneous method called functionalism. On the contrary, Davis claims, there is simply sociology, traceable from Robertson Smith and Durkheim, to its crystallization in Malinowski and Radcliffe-Brown. Davis allows that, when it began, functionalism was a distinct doctrine which set itself against various anti-scientific views abroad at the time. Now, he opines, it has been so stretched that it is co-extensive with sociology and social anthropology themselves. Such special features as it is alleged to have are merely the features of scientific method in general.

Hence, at what I have taken to be the high point of functionalism we have a grand claim for it: that it is co-extensive with sociological explanation. We also have a modest claim for it: there is nothing very special about functionalism; it may even be that, apart from terminology, it is not a distinct doctrine at all. Early on in this module functionalism was declared not to exist. This was not because Davis' position was to be adopted. But it is, nevertheless, interesting to see an arch-functionalist, placed in the position of expounding, defending, marking-off functionalism, declaring the whole dispute about its merits a pseudo-problem. Certainly this is an original explanation of the confusion surrounding discussions of functionalism: people think

---

[12] Talcott Parsons (1902-      ) recently retired from a professorship of sociology at Harvard University.
[13] Marion J. Levy (1918-      ) is a professor of sociology at Princeton University.
[14] Kingsley Davis (1908-      ) is a professor of sociology at the University of California, Berkeley.

it is something special and try to pin this down, but it is nothing special at all!

Even after Davis we find a functionalism of a Malinowskian cast being revived by Walter Goldschmidt[15] (an anthropologist) in his *Comparative Functionalism* of 1966. Repudiating as too limited the sociological functionalism of Radcliffe-Brown, he opts for viewing social systems as adaptive mechanisms for coping with both social and biological human needs. What anthropology must do is seek the universal imperatives of human and social existence. These functional requisites need to be postulated and then tested for. They can then be used to explain the particular forms societies take.

Ideally, from the point of view of scientific debate, the extensions and modifications to functionalism should have been discussed together. This has not been done because the original functionalists, Malinowski and Radcliffe-Brown, engaged in much controversy, where they defended fixed positions and scorned others, but in little genuine debate, where the object was to encourage criticism and to learn from it. Malinowski's ever-increasing interest in social biology seems to have been unaffected by the criticisms of the Radcliffe-Brown school, who were, in their turn, slow to take any account of social biology. (As late as 1963 Gellner was trying to explain to extreme Radcliffe-Brownians that we study kinship systems because they overlap in a systematic way with real physical bonds.) So far as I know, Davis' theory of stratification, Merton's manifest and latent, Parsons' entire system, etc., did not emerge in response to vigorous criticism. Davis' grand claims for functionalism were certainly an answer to critics — and what an answer.

Yet, I believe that valid criticisms were urged against functionalism and, if its adherents did not accept them overtly, they made surreptitious changes of position to come to terms with them. In some cases the critics themselves were highly sympathetic to functionalism and so attempted to revise it to meet their own criticisms. When, as with the papers by Lesser (1935) and Gregg and Williams (1948), replies were forthcoming from Radcliffe-Brown they were usually to the effect that he had been misunderstood.

(It should be added that Mary Douglas' theory of taboo, which we have looked at above, is a case of criticism bearing fruit. Radcliffe-Brown's theory of taboo as expressive of social value, was severely criticized by his pupil Franz Steiner. Mary Douglas, in turn, traces her ideas back to Steiner's suggestion, after criticizing Radcliffe-Brown, that rules of uncleanliness be set in the whole range of dangers in any given universe.)

[15] Walter Goldschmidt (1913-    ) is professor of anthropology at the University of California, Los Angeles.

# Modification
# Under Criticism

Even while functionalism was spreading and flourishing there were writers trying to write its obituary. It has been criticized for: reifying abstractions; stressing the static rather than dynamic aspects of society; being trite or circular; confusing cause with effect; introducing teleology or purpose; serving colonialism; being uncritical or unscientific; being anti-individualistic; etc. That is already a pretty long list of pretty serious criticisms and it is by no means exhaustive. If even half of them were true, even if only of particular functionalists rather than of functionalism itself, it is surprising that it continued to grow and even for a while flourish. The explanation can only be that the criticisms did not hit functionalism where it hurt, that its strengths and weaknesses to those teaching it and those accepting it were not directly dependent on the doctrines which were subject to criticism. This point has been hinted at before, but must be brought out more strongly now as we proceed to review the criticisms that have been made of functionalism in an attempt to understand both its strengths and its weaknesses. The point is that functionalism was not exhausted by its doctrine: it was also, if you like, a practice or method, and this aspect of it was far less often subject to criticism than the theories that apparently underpinned that method. Yet to practicing anthropologists this practical side was by far the most important. It is almost as if anthropologists, in responding to their critics' attacks on their theories, were saying, don't pay attention to what we say, or what you think we say, pay attention to what we do: that is functionalism. Rarely did the critics heed this plea — as we shall now see.

From the huge welter of critical literature we have selected a few items that seem to mark crucial articulations of important points and which have become standard contributions to the literature. To begin with, a paper in the *American Anthropologist* in 1935, "Functionalism in Social Anthropology," by Alexander Lesser[16] explains how functionalism arose as a reaction against

---

[16] Alexander Lesser (1902-    ) taught anthropology at Columbia.

evolutionism, how the reality of cultures was felt to be in their present and not in their past. He points out, however, that this repudiation of past history goes too far: "Is history to be impugned because of the errors in a particular conception of its nature?" The critique of evolutionism, Lesser observes, was anticipated by the German-American anthropologist, Franz Boas. But Boas did not turn aside from history as such. On the contrary, he pleaded for a proper historical anthropology which would have an empirical rather than a speculative basis. Boas wanted history to be reconstructed from what we know, not the facts fitted to preconceived theories. In general, Lesser argues, functionalists have too often identified rather narrow studies with correctness of method and content, and history with bad history. But "determining and fundamental relations only too often lie beyond the present in the past." What needs to supersede functionalism is "functional historicity" — which studies the reality of events and societies in the present, but which also takes account of

*... the fact that institutions, customs, beliefs, artifacts, have careers in time, and that their form and character is molded more by what has happened to them in the course of that history than by what particular things they occur associated with at any one time (1935, p. 393).*

Lesser's critique portends some of the points to be made in sharper and crisper form by Gellner (1958). Lesser cites absolutely no specific authors, so it is unclear whether he is talking about any of the individual anthropologists we have identified as functionalists. At the beginning of his paper he does identify functionalism with the study of patterns of attitude. Perhaps this is simply because he collapsed sociology and psychology in a way common at the time. Alternatively, he may have misunderstood Durkheim's notion of "sentiments," which might better have been translated as "dispositions."

A long silence ensued. Papers critical of functionalism may have appeared in the interim, but they did not make any impact. Obviously 1948 was a bad year for functionalism, for in addition to the attack launched on Malinowski by Gluckman, to which we shall come presently, there appeared an article in the *American Anthropologist* by Gregg and Williams[17] with the scathing title "The Dismal Science of Functionalism." The paper proceeds to dig out basic theoretical preconceptions behind functionalism and criticizes them, especially by showing how they parallel classical economic theory of the market. The authors begin with what they consider the concealed psychological premise of all functionalism. Why do human beings act as they do; which is the equilibrium point towards which their behavior tends? Answer: the satisfaction that accrues to individuals. Radcliffe-Brown calls it hedonism. If what

---

[17] Dorothy Gregg and Elgin Williams were economists.

social institutions do is satisfy men, then who could deny that these institutions are reasonable, necessary, and just? To say that these institutions are necessary is to say that they all contribute to the working of the community. This turns attention to the alleged purposes of institutions and away from their consequences. The functional purpose of a religion may be to reinforce social cohesion. Its consequence may be that it keeps its followers imprisoned in superstition and ignorance. Similarly, suppose an institution has a functional purpose; this may attract attention away from the fact that it is inefficient, that a different institution could do the job better. Hence functionalists endorse witchcraft and sorcery against modern medicine, primitive technology against advanced, and so on.

Functionalists also assume that simply because they exist societies are harmoniously functioning wholes. "Ceremonials are necessary to keep certain sentiments alive. 'Without the ceremonial these sentiments would not exist, and without them the social organization in its actual form would not exist.'" (Gregg and Williams, 1948, p. 601). What evidence exists for this notion of harmony? Why do functionalists ever talk of social sanctions if everything tends towards harmony? Is it not more plausible to say societies are characterized by an irrepressible tendency towards disequilibrium and rapid change?

Gregg and Williams go on to argue that the animism of the organic metaphor leads to confusion in situations of culture contact. A man cannot replace one of his limbs. So, when a culture takes over from another some trait or institution, the anthropologist declares the culture in its pristine form has gone.

Perhaps the most serious consequence of functionalism Gregg and Williams detect is the doctrine of cultural relativism. Cultures are uniquely expressive of the group or people, hence there are no universal standards of value or morals: whatever is is right. This sits ill with the facts of fascism and imperialism, slavery and racialism. What then does the functionalist do? He draws on liberal principles totally in conflict with his functionalism. Or, at least, some functionalists like Malinowski do. Others have greatly aided British colonial administration, the American administration of Japan, and so on. Others still have even had the temerity to argue that while life is hard among primitive peoples, they will be happier living in their societies than in one adapted after ours. This shocking series of accusations is carefully documented by Gregg and Williams and repays careful thought. Slavery, stratification, exploitation, ignorance, and so on have often been and sometimes still are institutionalized. Can a doctrine which suggests that the victims of all this will be happier, more secure, than with the "too many alternatives" available in western culture be excused? In the conclusion of the article the authors point out that we need to discriminate good from bad goals, stultifying from liberating institutions, efficient from inefficient customs.

19

Gregg's and Williams' paper annoyed even anthropologists critical of functionalism. It is difficult to see why. Relativism, antiquarianism, and colonialism were not accidentally part of the functionalist climate of opinion, however unfair the accusations may have seemed against anthroplogists as individuals.

Also in 1948, Max Gluckman[18] published two vitriolic attacks on Malinowski. The most acid dealt with Malinowski's theory of culture change. The other was on his functional theory. We shall concentrate on the latter. Gluckman's assault on Malinowski's functionalism carried weight not so much for itself but because it was a published manifestation of what had long been said within British anthropology. Gluckman was a South African (later a professor in England) trained by Radcliffe-Brown's pupils. The Radcliffe-Brownians had long felt Malinowski's theoretical position was untenable. Here at last was one of them explaining why in print. After praising Malinowski's theories for the impetus they gave to fieldwork and for the way they encouraged the fieldworker to see a primitive society as a whole, Gluckman attacks. Malinowski, he says, uses the word function equivocally; at least four separate meanings can be detected: satisfaction of need (marriage ensures reproduction); the relation between a group and the community (the Nuer lineage); the dependence of traits on the whole (the taboo on pork); the integration of institutions (the *kula*). Despite glimmerings, from time to time, Gluckman feels Malinowski never managed to see social life as a *system:* his holism should have led him that way, but his thought does not develop. Gluckman also shows that insofar as there is development it is towards more and more emphasis on the psychological and biological basis of society, rather than on the social level itself. Thus he feels the whole theory of basic needs is utterly trite.

*There appears to me to be little point in sending an anthropologist trained expensively and living at some cost in the field, to Africa to find out that some Bantu tribe has a complex organization to satisfy the need of its members for food, just as we have a complex organization for this purpose (p. 236).*

What does add to our knowledge is his description of tribal organization. Gluckman, then, is charging that functionalism of a Malinowskian kind is *trite* when it strays into psychology or biology. But even when it stays on a sociological level, it can easily become tautological (repeating the same thing in another way). Gluckman cites the legend of a student of Malinowski's who is supposed to have ended a thesis with, "Our survey of the facts has forced us to conclude that the function of leadership in primitive societies is to

[18] Max Gluckman (1911-    ) was born in South Africa and became professor of anthropology in the Victoria University of Manchester.

initiate and organize activities." Gluckman goes on to quote a passage from Malinowski himself that is just about as tautological.

All these criticisms will seem straightforward enough. They hit Malinowski pretty hard, and it is difficult to see how a functionalist of his particular ilk could reply. There is in addition a more controversial criticism, which raises an issue in the philosophy of science. This is that Gluckman attacks Malinowski's view that fieldwork *descriptions* constitute the science of anthropology: "Explanation to the scientific thinker is nothing else but the most complete description of a complex fact" (Gluckman, p. 239, quoting Malinowski). Following Radcliffe-Brown, Gluckman wants to argue that science seeks not mere descriptions but laws as the basis of its explanation. Clearly there will be no laws of individual societies. To discover laws, different societies will have to be compared. The laws will be general. But in order to compare societies, they have to be seen not just as wholes but as systems, because, while systems are wholes, their parts can be analytically distinguished, discussed, and generalized about. Upon laws reached in this manner can a science of society be built.

Some of these criticisms hit only at functionalism in its Malinowskian form; others, such as those of triteness and tautology, cut a broader swathe. This becomes clear when we turn to a more famous critic, although not an anthropologist, but similarly one who argues from inside functionalism, both as an advocate and practitioner. Robert K. Merton (1957) attempted a comprehensive review and restatement of functionalism in the same chapter of *Social Theory and Social Structure* which makes the distinction between manifest and latent functions. The criticisms he produces are more cases of functionalists unknowingly painting themselves into a corner, when they could easily avoid doing so.

Merton too begins with the multitudinous uses of the word "function"; he distinguishes five: a social occasion; an occupation; assigned duties; a relationship in mathematics between two or more variables; a vital process contributing to the maintenance of a system. Only the latter sense, he concludes, is relevant to sociology and anthropology. He then proceeds to detect three postulates which underlie such sociological functionalism, each of which needs to be modified. The first postulate is that society is a functional unity, or it is integrated. He points out that many organisms are poorly integrated or organized and can either replace, or survive without some of, their parts. It would therefore seem quite possible that more complex systems like society could also be loosely organized. However, he is prepared to concede that many of the small, non-literate societies studied by anthropologists might be classified as functional unities. One might add that the evidence from contact situations where western technology, economics, values, and religion are offered to primitive societies, is that destructive effects almost invariably follow. Merton concludes that the unit or system for which a given social

21

item is functional must be specified, and the possibility of diverse consequences, functional and dysfunctional, for the individual, for subgroups, and
for the society as a whole must be allowed for.

The second postulate which Merton exposes and criticizes is the postulate of universal functionalism, the doctrine that every social and cultural
item fulfills some vital function in the society in which it appears. If this is
true by definition Merton does not quarrel with it; if it is an heuristic injunc-
tion to search for functions he would accept that, too. But he does not accept
that the quarrel over survivals justifies a reaction to such an extreme position.
Let me explain. Many anthropologists of the late nineteenth and early
twentieth centuries spent time discussing cultural items (such as the buttons
on the sleeve of a man's suit) or social items which were felt to be out of
date, to have survived from an earlier time when they had some function. On
the basis of such survivals, many conjectural schemes of human development
were devised. Malinowski argued that social and cultural items could not be
plucked from their social or cultural context in this way and maintained that
if they had survived they must perform some function. Merton denies this,
affirms there are survivals, and says we can only allow that persisting social
forms must have a *net balance* of functional consequences.

The third postulate, and perhaps the most dangerous, is that of indispensability: not only that every part of society has a function, but that every
part is indispensable. An ambiguity is hidden here: is it, as it were, that the
*kula* is indispensable or is it that the function the *kula* performs (social
integration) is indispensable? Merton argues that "just as the same item may
have multiple functions, so may the same function be diversely fulfilled by
alternative items" (pp.33-34).

Finally, Merton defends functionalism from the charges that it favors
conservative ideology, or that it favors radical ideology. The former charge
points to the functionalist interest in how society currently works and what it
needs to survive. The latter charge points out how functionalism doesn't
allow things like religion, magic, or the *kula* value in and for themselves alone.
Rather must their persistence be explained in terms of other values, some-
what collectivist (social survival) values, at that. To all this Merton is able to
respond that functionalism, in its moderated form as he has expounded it, is
ideologically neutral, able to be employed by both conservatives and radicals.

Merton's critique of functionalism was of considerable value, as its conceptual distinction between manifest and latent functions clarified a good
many issues. In particular it laid the groundwork for disposal of the so-called
teleological issue by Hempel, a decade later. We shall come to that presently.
Moreover, it drew attention to a key difference between social systems and
the organic systems we call organisms. Whereas all functions in organisms (of
the heart, other organs, etc.) are latent, it is only in human systems that you
get manifest functions; it is only humans who consciously and deliberately

act to achieve certain goals or ends. This makes the application of evolutionary theory to society (known as social Darwinism) very tricky because goals or purposes upset the whole notion of the survival of the fittest guiding the course of development like a hidden hand. It also lays the groundwork for an even stronger thesis essayed by Hayek that, since human actions have both intended and unintended consequences, the social sciences should concentrate on those that are unintended: only those, as it were, need explaining. We cannot pursue that point here.

A couple of years later, in 1951, the Yale anthropologist G.P. Murdock[19] published a critique of "British Social Anthropology" in the *American Anthropologist*. Many of his arguments are directed against the functionalists as a group rather than at their theory. But since by then practically all British anthropologists were functionalists, his arguments struck at theory too. His thesis was that functionalism has made British anthropologists not anthropologists at all, but sociologists who study primitive societies. There was more than name-calling to this criticism. Murdock noted that functionalism in the form espoused by Radcliffe-Brown and his followers had no use for what he claims to be the central concept of anthropology, namely culture. Technology, folklore, art, child training, and even language being almost completely ignored by functionalists. In fact, he noted, functionalists tend to concentrate on kinship and areas connected with kinship, namely government, religion, (and, he might have added) land tenure. True enough, one might say, but is it necessary for functionalism to be like that, are these criticisms more of the way it is practiced and of its practical effects than of the doctrine itself? We shall have more to say on the centrality of kinship studies in our concluding section.

In strong contrast to Lesser, Murdock also slates British functionalists for their indifference to psychology, as well as culture. Indeed, sometimes the thrust of his critique seems to be that British anthropologists are at fault because they do not do what the American anthropologists think they ought to do. This comes out particularly when he praises Radcliffe-Brown's American pupil Eggan for fusing functionalism with an interest in history and the process of change. These are two key charges he lays against functionalism. However, he is not simply saying that functionalists have not done historical studies or studies of change. He goes further and argues that this is no accident.

Murdock maintains that functionalism directs attention to the way a social system connects up, rather than how those entities connected and their connections came about over time. This leads to a neglect of history and a failure to study social change. Still, one may ask, is this not more a matter of predilection than of design? No, according to Murdock, because Radcliffe-

---

[19] George Peter Murdock (1897-    ) was professor of anthropology at Yale.

Brown taught functionalists to search for social laws, but he argued that these laws could be found by intensive study of a very few societies selected without reference to their representativeness. This Murdock calls a serious distortion of scientific method. He also says that these laws are expressed without specification of the concomitant behavior of variables. Once a connection

*...has been tentatively established, the ethnographer, being inhibited from seeking any connection through such factors as psychology or process, is tempted to convert his discovery into a cause-and-effect relationship (p. 470).*

That is not clearly expressed, but seems to mean that the system being studied is not clearly specified and so neither are the factors which influence it. This too portends a criticism we shall encounter later in Brown (1963).

In 1958 E.A. Gellner,[20] a British philosopher, trained in anthropology, published a paper in the philosophical journal *Mind* which levelled a number of criticisms at functionalism, while overall defending it. These criticisms were elaborated and developed in later papers. Fundamentally, the thesis Gellner has maintained is that as a doctrine functionalism is mistaken, as a method it is salutary. Against functionalism he has argued as follows: the preoccupation of functionalists with the truth that every social item is to some extent functional has obscured the even more important truth that some things are far more functional than others. Even the organisms on analogy with which so much functionalism turns, have functionless tails and appendices. It needs no great leap of imagination to think that societies might have such redundant parts as well. To suggest that all societies are finely tuned and completely functional is grotesque; to say that many things in society connect up with many others in complicated and unexpected ways is obvious. Somewhere between absurdity and trivial truth the interesting truth must lie, but functionalism is semi-vacuous because it fails to say just where. Moreover, when the extreme formulation is adopted social change becomes not only inexplicable, but unimaginable, unless exogenously induced (but then, a perfectly harmonious society should be immune to outside infection). A consequence is the way functionalists deride history. They believe each social item stands in a context and only that context should be used to explain that item. The present explains the present; the past explains nothing. Again, there is good methodological advice here, but as a doctrine it won't hold up. A number of arguments: if a past moment won't explain a present moment, why should a present moment explain itself? What is the justification for such privileged moments? Secondly, in fact history is presupposed. Extreme functionalism sets out to explain the maintenance of stability or

---

[20] Ernest André Gellner (1925-    ) is professor of philosophy at the London School of Economics.

equilibrium. But what else does this mean than that the society under discussion has a stable history which is now to be explained (presumably by enduring rather than instantaneously present features). In his later developments Gellner (1962, 1967) concludes that functionalism is best regarded as a method of seeking non-superficial causal explanations of social phenomena, and that this method happens to have been framed in a rather overstated doctrine mainly because of the debates that were taking place in anthropology at the time it was formulated. These debates, as we have seen, sifted rather haphazardly accumulated reports on societies all over the world for oddities (survivals), and then sought to fit these oddities into a pattern either of evolution or of diffusion from a center. The functionalist polemics against such historical interests and against ever thinking a fact about society could be analytically discussed may have been hysterical. But what emerged was an enriched anthropology which seemed genuinely able to explain why things happened. Gellner points out that if functionalist explanations are read backwards, they become perfectly respectable attempts at causal explanation. To say of the *kula* that it promotes the cohesion of widely scattered island societies, is simply to give an explanation of that cohesion. In its turn the *kula* will be explained by other institutions, which function to maintain the *kula* (the institutions which see to it that ceremonies are remembered, preparations begun in time, labor and materials assembled when they are needed, and so on and so on; in fact, much of the contents of Malinowski's fat book).

Gellner's distinction between functionalism as doctrine and functionalism as method, his indication of the problems of even formulating it as doctrine in such a way that it is not dismissed out of hand, and his suggestions towards a refined and moderate version of it were the first of a series of contributions by philosophers. In 1958 a book by Emmett appeared, followed in rapid succession by pieces by Hempel, Nagel, Brown, and Jarvie. Only the last of the critics we shall look at, Marvin Harris, is a fullfledged anthropologist.

In a patient and cogent paper, the philosopher of science Carl G. Hempel[21] examined "The Logic of Functional Analysis" in 1959. He begins by attempting to get at the logic of functionalism as explanation. Let us reconstruct his abstractions by using the *kula* as an illustration.

(a) At time $t$, the system of islands $s$ known as the *kula* ring functions adequately in a setting of kind $c$.
(b) $s$ functions adequately in a setting of kind $c$ only if the necessary condition $n$ of maintenance and integration is satisfied.

---

[21] Carl G. Hempel (1905-    ) is professor of philosophy at Princeton University.

(c) If there were trait *i* (a periodic religious ceremony) to reinforce this integration then *n* would be satisfied.

---

(d) Hence at *t*, trait *i* is present in *s*.

Hempel points out that this argument is not formally valid. It commits the fallacy of affirming the consequent in regard to conditional premise *(c)*. (The fallacy of affirming the consequent can be simply illustrated, for example if someone argues from the fact that the streets are wet and the premise, if it is raining then the streets will be wet, to the conclusion that therefore it has been raining. The conclusion doesn't follow. It may have been a sunny day and the city chose to hose down the streets.) *(d)* would follow from *(a)*, *(b)*, and *(c)* only if *(c)* said that *only* trait *i* could satisfy necessary condition *n*. As it is, all we can infer is that:

*(d')* At *t*, some trait must be present in *s* to satisfy *n*.

This really amounts to no more than saying, if the streets are wet then *something* must have wet them. If the *kula* ring stays an integrated whole, something must integrate it. Hardly profound. Hempel notes that Malinowski sometimes suggests that a trait like magic is indispensable, at other times he allows that there may be a limited range of possibilities, or functional equivalents. We recall that Merton, on whom Hempel draws, attacked the postulate of functional indispensability and replaced it with that of functional alternatives. Suppose, then, that the islands in the *kula* ring replaced the *kula* ceremony with closed-circuit TV links between all the islands, and periodic conferences to discuss island problems and gossip. Would these then constitute functional alternatives to the *kula*? An anthropologist who argued in the negative, to the effect that the internal and external conditions of the system *s* were so different that it was no longer the same system, and that there was no functional equivalent to the *kula* which would leave the essential features of the group unimpaired, is then turning the functional indispensability postulate into a tautology, immune to any attempts to refute it empirically.

Turning to the possibility of making predictions using functional analysis, Hempel argues that a cautious prediction of the kind that states, "if system *s* functions adequately, then there must be a trait or traits satisfying each of its necessary conditions," is about all that functionalism can muster. When functionalists go further and argue from a statement of functional prerequisite (integration, say) to a categorical assertion that some trait will be found, trouble develops. For the predictors are committed to asserting some lawlike statement to the effect that systems of this and this kind will develop appropriate traits in response to changes in their internal state or external environment. This Hempel dubs the hypothesis of self-regulation. Fair enough, he concedes, but such a hypothesis must be reasonably definite and open to empirical test. He quotes Radcliffe-Brown:

*. . .it may be that we should say that . . . a society thrown into a condition of functional disunity or inconsistency . . . will not die, except in such comparatively rare instances as an Australian tribe overwhelmed by the white man's destructive force, but will continue to struggle toward . . . some kind of social health . . . (Radcliffe-Brown, 1952, p. 183).*

But the "except" clause is deceptive. What now constitutes a clear-cut test? What is to prevent the anthropologist from saying that the very fact a society "died" is evidence that the disruptive forces were overwhelming? These problems result from vagueness about the scope of the self-regulation hypothesis.

Further problems arise because of non-empirical specification of such functionalist terms as "need," "adequate functioning," and so on. This criticism cuts deeper because it goes back to point out fundamental difficulties even in the weak explanatory and predictive inferences already discussed. Needs could, for example, be relativized to survival, thus: unless the needs or requisites of the society are met, it will not survive. But then, we must have some specification of what it is for such a system to live, what its normal or equilibrium state of living is like, how it is to be recognized and tested for. This has hardly been done, and the result is quite diverse subjective interpretations of "need" statements. It is also possible to relativize the functional requisites of the society less to its survival and more to its adaptation or adjustment. Or perhaps to its maintenance of the unity of the social system.

*We may define it as a condition in which all parts of the social system work together with a sufficient degree of harmony or internal consistency, i.e., without producing persistent conflicts which can neither be resolved nor regulated (Radcliffe-Brown, 1952, p. 181).*

Concepts like "adjustment" and "unity" are as vague and open to subjective assessment as "survival." There is a temptation to make them tautological by construing any response of the given system as "adjustment" or "contributing to unity." None of these concepts will be more than suggestive until they are spelled out properly.

Hempel also looks at the accusation of teleology and has little difficulty in disposing of it. Functionalism need not postulate the future state (of functional integration or whatever) as a final cause of what is happening in the present. Rather does functionalism attribute a disposition to the system as now constituted, to respond to certain changes in certain ways. The attraction of functionalism may, Hempel thinks, have something to do with its *apparent* attribution of purposes, but in fact that is only legitimate with respect to purposive behavior. If the analogy is with the systems studied in biology then, it should be noted, purpose is not there assumed. Hempel ends his paper by commenting that this exposure of weaknesses, vagueness, and

27

tautology does not detract from the heuristic value of functionalism. We shall attend closely to this point later.

Two years later, in 1961, another philosopher of science, Ernest Nagel,[22] included a chapter on functionalism in his major text *The Structure of Science*. After distinguishing at least six separate meanings of the word function he launches his critique. To begin with, he notes that in biology functional explanations presuppose a system and a state of the system which is maintained. Usually the system is an organism, the state maintained is life. But societies are difficult to demarcate as systems, and moreover they may disappear, but they don't die (or get sick). If survival is merely the continuance of some humans in some groups then functionalism is compatible with any form of organization and hence is tautologous. Suppose an attempt is made to sharpen this up. Let's say, to survive a society must exhibit a political organization. If "political organization" is interpreted widely as any means of social control, then no society is without it; if it is interpreted narrowly, as centralized state monopoly of force, bureaucracy, etc., then many societies studied by anthropologists, such as the Nuer, do not have it. Moreover, they not only survive, they thrive.

Similar difficulties arise if Radcliffe-Brown's notion of an unchanging structure of social relations is used. What it amounts to for the various kinds of social relations to remain the same is desperately vague. Some order will always be exhibited by any collection of events. But what empirical criteria have we for kinds of social relations and for their remaining the same? Nagel asks whether, if a state nationalizes its industry its social structure is the same. In one sense, the answer is no because state monopoly has replaced private capitalism; but in the sense that this is still an industrialized society and people still work on production lines, etc., the answer is yes.

Nagel concludes that specification of the relevant system and the relevant state of the system is essential — but also difficult. Functionalism will be untestable unless, when a function is attributed to a particular variable, say the *kula* ceremony, the Nuer lineage, or to magic, that function is made relative *to a particular system*. It has also to be conceded that that variable may not be the only one contributing towards the maintenance of the relevant state of the system. Both the thyroid glands and the adrenal glands regulate the temperature of the human body, and some bodies function quite well with the thyroid surgically removed. This sort of example needs to be borne in mind when functional necessity or indispensability is discussed.

In 1963 another philosopher, Robert Brown,[23] had a chapter on function in his excellent text *Explanation in Social Science*. He argues that the model behind structural functionalism is a so-called negative feedback system,

---

[22] Ernest Nagel (1901-    ) was professor of philosophy at Columbia University.
[23] Robert Brown teaches philosophy at the Australian National University.

like a thermostat which maintains the temperature of a building at a certain level. Successfully to apply this idea to the social sciences requires, he says, that three clear conditions be satisfied. We must know: what property is being maintained in a steady state; what internal properties are the variables, how can they be measured, and what are their values and ranges; and which external conditions are assumed to be constant and which to vary within specifiable limits. If we recall the *kula* we see that it is a pretty tall order to meet all these requirements. The property is social solidarity. The internal variables are the marks of solidarity or its lack. The external conditions are presumably those which tend to threaten the solidarity unless it is reinforced. We see at once that the whole explanation dissolves into vagueness. If we accept Gellner's point that functional explanations are merely causal explanations written backwards, well and good. But if we seriously try to maintain that the *kula* ring is a social structure or system, the state of solidarity of which is maintained by the *kula* ceremony, we will have arrived nowhere. Nothing is explained, and nothing is testable.

This failure to explain is perhaps the most serious criticism of functionalism that can be launched. Let me now ruminate upon it. If the problem is, why do the Trobrianders have the *kula,* then clearly, "to reinforce the social solidarity of the island societies in the *kula* ring," is not much of an answer. Social solidarity may be an interesting *consequence* of the *kula* ceremonies, but processes are not usually thought to be explained by their consequences. Perhaps we have first to ask, what do we want an explanation for, anyway? If we see some Christians in a church at harvest time do we demand an explanation? If we do, then we will be told they are there to thank the Supreme Being in which they believe for a good harvest. Again, that their foregathering may have the useful effect of reinforcing community bonds is interesting but not explanatory. Why will not a similar explanation do for the *kula?* Part of the answer, I fear, is that the *kula* appears to be an elaborate expenditure of wealth and energy with no apparent point. Why all that fuss to trade in useless and valueless decorative objects? Not just because they happen to believe in it as a tradition handed down from time immemorial? Might one not ask why it was once fashionable in Christianity to spend much wealth and energy on long and difficult pilgrimages to holy places? Shall one answer about how the ties of communication, and hence the cohesion of Christendom, were thereby buttressed? Or does it not seem more straightforward simply to talk of people who believe in certain things acting upon those beliefs?

This is where Merton comes into his own. It is the latent functions of customs, not their manifest functions, that we seek. No individual designed and controls the *kula.* It is the unintended consequence of the separate actions of men in widely scattered societies. It comes about though no one intends it to. We then study it as a partial explanation of how the system of island societies in the *kula* ring are harmoniously interdependent. Similarly, a confluence of buyers and sellers results in what economists call a market. This can then be studied as part of the explanation of the workings of the economy.

Taking up from Hempel and Brown, in my own contribution to the critical debate I maintained first that functional explanations were not logically valid; and second that functional difficulties with social change were neither accidental nor avoidable. The second point was illustrated by means of the study of Melanesian cargo cults. Basically the problem was this. South Sea Island societies are fairly isolated and could easily be demarcated as systems. Also, they seem fairly tradition-bound and stable. However, over the last ninety years they have been convulsed by religious revival movements called cargo cults. These were a mixture of various western rites and ideas (religious and secular) but grafted onto characteristic Melanesian notions of the sudden improvement and perfection of the society. At first the cults were explained by imagining that the "savages" had gone mad. Then it was assumed that they were simply garbling up the fragments of western culture to which they were unsystematically exposed. The way they behaved was hardly functional, since destroying crops and expending massive amounts of labor on useless construction was not conducive to survival or stability. Noting that prophets and untraditional leadership patterns emerged (there is no chieftainship in Melanesia), and the obvious impact of imperialism and colonialism, Marxists sought to explain the cults as part of the process of throwing off colonial oppression and the formation of class-consciousness. But the key point is the failure of functionalism. While the system may be specifiable, the state of it that is being maintained cannot be, especially as the cults come and go and the society survives their convulsions. Indeed, there is evidence that religious convulsions are part of the Melanesian religious *tradition*. It is hard to see this as a steady state. Yet obviously also the cults are a response to the impact of external forces in the wider world — the clash of cultures. The external (or exogenous) variables obviously cannot be held constant, since the impact of missionaries, planters, businessmen, troops, not to mention mail packet boats on the island societies, is highly irregular. So neither functional imperatives of Melanesia nor functional imperatives of the western world will explain cargo cults. A complex economic, political, historical, sociological, and even philosophical story is the minimum that will explain cargo cults. Some argue that perhaps a functional explanation of cargo cults is impossible, but that functionalism, with its emphasis on context and interdependence, will greatly aid the tracing-out of the consequential development and impact of the cults. This is so, and throws up once again the important distinction between functionalism as a theory and functionalism as a method. We shall take this up properly in the last chapter.

A final critic of functionalism deserves to be looked at — the American anthropologist Marvin Harris,[24] who recently wrote a weighty tome on the history of anthropology. Harris' (1968) criticisms are unusual in that they come from a well-developed alternative point of view to functionalism. He calls it cultural materialism, and it might be described as the view the social systems are natural systems of adaptation to the facts of the struggle for survival in a harsh physical environment, and that what anthropology studies is how these forces shape the cultures which inhabit them. Harris heartily approves of Radcliffe-Brown's idea that anthropology should be a science of society, and he even casts a sympathetic glance at the attempt to formulate laws of social systems. However, he cites a passage in which the question is posed, not, how do kinship systems work, but, why does a particular society have matrilineal rather than patrilineal organization? Radcliffe-Brown simply confesses inability to cope with this question. So, functionalism does not explain why things are the way they are, only, given the way they are, how they work. Harris then goes on to look at "dynamic" theory, that is functionalist attempts to explain social change. Again he is able to show that they get nowhere. The reasons are those we saw with cargo cults. Much social change is not explainable in terms of the social structure. Some is caused by the impact of external events, other is caused, for Harris, by shifts or changes in the environment. Malinowski, Harris feels, was much closer to being on the correct track in his search for the cultural determinants (or basic needs) which all societies must cope with. But, to return to the *kula*, Malinowski does not carry out his ideas.

*We learn only incidentally, never in detail, that the whimsical voyagers circulate not only arm bands and necklaces but coconuts, sago, fish, vegetables, baskets, mats, sword clubs, green stone (formerly essential for tools), mussel shells (for knives), and creepers (essential for lashings) (p. 63).*

But Malinowski subordinates all this to the Trobrianders' own feeling that the ceremonial of the *kula* is what counts. Harris comments:

*We are thrown back upon the ethnosemantic categories and subjective psychological appraisals and reactions of the actors, who constitute those elements in the whole array least capable of comprehending the socio-cultural system to which they have been conditioned. We are henceforth denied a picture of the whole system as it moves through time, related to an island habitat, rich in ecological specialties, fluctuating in population, variable in annual production, precarious for human existence during droughts, typhoons, and war, and progressively subject to European blackbirding, pearl diving, and copra trading (1968, p. 64).*

[24] Marvin Harris (1927-      ) is professor of anthropology at Columbia University.

*Functionalism*

Harris, in other words, is closer to Mary Douglas than to Malinowski. Where Douglas takes off from the basic fact of the Israelites as a pastoralist society, and suggests that this way of life was their standard of what was correct, and that taboos proceeded from that, Harris maintains that the *kula* is a trade system of the greatest economic importance which has been surrounded with ceremonial and magic. To concentrate on the latter is to miss the point. Recent works by Uberoi (1962), Brookfield and Hart (1971), and Wax (1972), lend support to Harris. Curiously, this sort of explanation would have pleased Malinowski, and annoyed Durkheim and Radcliffe-Brown. Social events are seen as integrated with ecology (pastoralism, pig-keeping), economy (trade), the political situation (colonialism), religious beliefs (theirs and the missionaries), and all must be marshalled to explain them. If this is a far cry from the functionalism so long dominant and in dispute, it is nevertheless interesting that functionalism and the criticism of functionalism can be seen to have paved the way.

# Assessment

Clearly, underlying all functional doctrines is the fundamental metaphor of the living organism, its several parts and organs, grouped and organized into a system, the function of the various parts and organs being to sustain the organism — to keep its essential processes going and enable it to reproduce. Society can be thought of along these sorts of lines. Its members can be looked upon as cells, its institutions as organs, whose function is to sustain the life of the collective entity, despite the frequent death of cells and production of new ones. Malinowski is very clearly aware of this metaphor, and in his later writing tries, in drawing up a list of basic needs necessary to human life, to relate the biology of the cells to the system of social organization. Radcliffe-Brown, too, was fond of this metaphor, but he was not fond of the theory that the function of society was to satisfy basic needs. He was more concerned to spell out the social function of the institutions — especially their latent functions. For him, society was a structure there before the people (cells) were born and continuing after they died. That there was life apart from society he would hardly have denied. Why then did basic needs not interest him? That human beings have organs of ingestion and reproduction does not explain how they feed and reproduce. This requires invocation of the entire biological and social systems in which they operate. Similarly the functioning and continuity of the society did not turn on the fact that they had means of satisfying basic needs. They turned on the cohesion and solidarity of the system. To understand this it was necessary to look at the parts and the way they connected up. This in turn could be illuminated by drawing contrasts with other social structures (social systems), similar and dissimilar.

The organic metaphor is a profound one, as old as Aristotle. But at the societal level it can be very misleading. In the matter of functionalism the key problems turn on the notions of system and of feedback. When we say of an organ or of a cog that it has a function, we are able to specify of what that function is a function. The function of the heart is to pump the blood — the blood of the body to which the heart belongs. In saying of the heart that it has this function, we are also able to say what would happen were the heart to falter or cease. Were it to falter, the body or system would be seriously disturbed and, unless the faltering were corrected, could die, i.e., cease to exist as an organized system. Hence the function of the heart is to help sustain the body-system in a certain living and stable state. When the body needs more blood, the heart speeds up, when it needs less, as in sleep, it slows down. The system's equilibrium, its ability to continue living (getting and eating food, eliminating, resting, reproducing, etc.), is sustained by various organs like the heart, each of which operates on negative feedback.

When we talk of the function of the *kula* and we ask, of what system is this a function, and what state of the system does the feedback sustain, the answers look obvious, but are not. The chain of Pacific islands which participate in the *kula* might be compared to a system. What state of that system does the *kula* maintain? The question is circular: the *kula* *is* the system; it sustains itself. (Compare: the function of the heart is to keep the heart functioning.) What, then, if the *kula* should falter or cease. The *kula* system would cease. And then what? Alternative trade routes and connections would have to be found, islands might seek other means to a harmonious coexistence. But then again they might not. Will their inhabitants die? Why should they? A human being cannot live without a heart or, at least, a blood pump, but societies can certainly continue to sustain themselves and their members without a *kula*.

This pretty well puts paid to Malinowski's attempt to link functionalism with the problem of human survival. Were he to have argued that, while the *kula* may not be necessary to survival, some institutions which facilitate and regulate food, work, rest, and reproduction are necessary, the answer would be that, of course, conditions for survival are necessary conditions for survival. His functionalism becomes a tautology. This often-made criticism is not altogether fair. Just because we know people survive, it does not follow that we know how they do it and hence have nothing to learn.

Malinowski's tautology, in fact, turns out to be one of the most fruitful aspects of his functionalism, for it challenges us to show how societies do manage the problem of survival and harmonious living in particular cases. We don't need to worry about the boundaries of the system particularly, but instead we can concentrate on mapping it and then on grasping its workings.

Strangely enough this is also the most fruitful core of Radcliffe-Brown's ideas. Radcliffe-Brown answered differently the questions about system and feedback. Systems were to be defined by their units and the special relations between the units (1957, p. 26). The units are human beings, the relations social. Anthropologists study such systems in a certain limited region during a certain period of time (1958, p. 167). What they seek, by observation, classification, and comparison, is the structural laws which society obeys. But what

societies "savage," etc. They also test the stronger hypothesis that we can make sense of everything that happens in alien societies. This hypothesis is clearly false — we can't even make sense of everything that happens in our own society. But we can and must continue in the attempt.

# Bibliography

Bendix, Reinhard, and Lipset, Seymour Martin, eds., 1966, *Class, Status, and Power,* New York: The Free Press.

Brookfield, H.C., and Hart, Doreen, 1971, *Melanesia, A Geographical Interpretation of an Island World,* London: Methuen.

Brown, Robert, 1963, *Explanation in Social Science,* London: Routledge.

Davis, Kingsley, and Moore, Wilbert E., 1945, "Some Principles of Stratification," *American Sociological Review,* vol. 10, pp. 242-247; reprinted in Bendix and Lipset.

Davis, Kingsley, 1959, "The Myth of Functional Analysis as a Special Method in Sociology and Anthropology," *American Sociological Review,* vol. 24, pp. 757-772; reprinted in Demerath and Peterson, pp. 379-402, page references to the latter.

Demerath III, N.J., and Peterson, Richard A., eds., 1967, *System, Change, and Conflict,* A Reader on Contemporary Sociological Theory and the Debate Over Functionalism, New York: The Free Press.

Douglas, Mary, 1966, *Purity and Danger,* London: Routledge.

Durkheim, Emile, 1912, *The Elementary Forms of the Religious Life,* translated by J.W. Swain, New York: Collier Books, 1961.

Eggan, Fred, ed., 1955, *Social Anthropology of North American Tribes,* Chicago: University of Chicago Press.

Emmet, D.M., 1958, *Function, Purpose and Powers,* London: Macmillan.

Evans-Pritchard, E.E., 1940, *The Nuer,* Oxford: Oxford University Press.

Fortes, Meyer, 1953, "The Structure of Unilineal Descent Groups," *American Anthropologist,* vol. 55, pp. 17-44.

Frazer, J.G., 1922, *The Golden Bough,* abridged edition, London: St. Martin's Library, 1957. (Original editions 1890 and 1911-1915.)

Gellner, E.A., 1958, "Time and Theory in Social Anthropology," *Mind,* vol. 67, pp. 182-202.

_____ .1962, "Concepts and Society," *Transactions of the Fifth World Congress of Sociology,* vol. 1, pp. 153-183.

# Functionalism

## I.C. JARVIE

I.C. Jarvie is presently a professor in the Department of Philosophy at
University, Ontario, Canada. He received his doctorate at the London S
of Economics. Dr. Jarvie has been a lecturer in philosophy at the Univ
of Hong Kong, as well as a visiting professor at Tufts University and B
University. His books include *The Revolution in Anthropology*, 1969, F
Regnery Company; *Movies and Society*, 1970, Basic Books, Inc.; and
*Story of Social Anthropology*, 1972, McGraw-Hill Book Company.

## Basic Concepts in Anthropology

### Consulting Editors:

**A. J. Kelso,** University of Colorado at Boulder
**Aram Yengoyan,** University of Michigan

Forthcoming Titles

Michael H. Agar: Cognition and Ethnography
Daniel Bates: Pastoralism
Richard K. Beardsley: Art and Anthropology
Gerald Broce: History of Anthropology
Stanley M. Garn: On-Going Human Evolution
John Greenway: Ethnomusicology
Robert Harrison: Warfare
Gordon W. Hewes: Origin of Man
Kenneth A. R. Kennedy: Neanderthal
Kenneth A. R. Kennedy: Paleodemography
George E. McLellan: Urban Archaeology
Laurence H. Snyder: Blood Groups*
Robert F. G. Spier: Material Culture and Technology
Gary G. Tunnell: Culture and Biology
Leslie A. White with Beth Dillingham: The Concept of Culture*
Aram A. Yengoyan: Cultural Ecology
Aram A. Yengoyan: Hunters and Gatherers

*Now available

**Burgess Publishing Company** • **Minneapolis, Minnesota**